THE MERCILESS MISSION OF MOLLY McCLOY

To Amy, Jo, Joanna, John, Miranda, Simon, Will

Also by Ian Grant

PLAYS
After the Ball
Stella Europa

LIBRETTO
Thomas Boleyn

SOCIAL HISTORY
The City at War
The Countryside at War

The Merciless Mission
of Molly McCloy

by Ian Grant

Cornwall Editions

First published 2021
by Cornwall Editions Ltd
52 Gladsmuir Road,
London N19 3JU

ISBN 978-1-904880-37-0

All professional enquiries regarding this play
should be addressed to:

Creative Structure Ltd,
52 Gladsmuir Road,
Upper Holloway,
London N19 3JU, UK

www.creativestructure.net
ian.grant@creativestructure.net

+44 776 418 7452

Cover design by Steven Maddocks
Cover photo: Creative Commons, Pixabay

The first performance of *The Merciless Mission of Molly McCloy* was given on 26 June 2020, played live on Zoom and livestreamed to Vimeo for broadcast online.

Cast, in alphabetical order

Paul Ansdell	Sean Smallwood
	and Albert LeFèvre
Rachael Mae Brady	Molly McCloy
Mark Carlisle	Sergey Igorovich Susemilh
Grace Cookey-Gam	Serena Ridinghard
Simon Lenagan	Freddie Branscombe MP

Creative crew

Director	**Ian Grant**

Assistant Director	Steven Maddocks
Sound design and operation	Philip Matejtschuk
Props and costumes	Amy Hunter
Marketing Manager	Amy Hunter
Graphic Design	Steven Maddocks
Producer	Ian Grant
Executive Producers	Niall Bishop, Ian Grant

Warm thanks to Niall Bishop, Alison Burns, John Retallack, Brian Walker

The Merciless Mission of Molly McCloy was produced by

TIME Productions

TIME AND SETTING
The immediate future, in Westminster and Wandsworth.

CHARACTERS
Molly McCloy, aged 33, Northern Irish Free Presbyterian Ulster
    Unionist spy
The Right Hon Freddie Branscombe, MP, aged 55, British Prime
    Minister
Dame Serena Ridinghard, aged 55, Head of MI5
Sean Smallwood, aged 43, middle-ranking DUP official and Special
    Operations Executive. Smallwood *masquerades as*
Albert LeFèvre, couturier
Sergey Igorovich Susemihl, Russian 'diplomat'

Molly and Sean have broad Northern Irish accents. Freddie and
Serena are RP. Albert Lefèvre has a cod French accent. Sergey
Susemihl has a sophisticated Moscow accent.

TEXT NOTES
A forward slash (/) followed by text indicates that the next line
overlaps the text after the slash. A gap between lines indicates a
pause; the larger the gap the longer the pause.

<h1 style="text-align:center">Act 1, Scene 1</h1>

Early evening. MOLLY's bed-sit in Wandsworth. A window, upstage centre, looks onto a blank wall. Drop-down bed to one side of window. Table to other side, suggestion of kitchen worksurface, cupboards beneath. Door on both sides of stage, one to exterior, other internal.

Music.

MOLLY is dressing and dancing. FREDDIE comes from the bathroom. Music stops instantly.

MOLLY: No, Freddie, you can't fuck me now.

FREDDIE: Look, I must, I've only got a few minutes.

MOLLY: I'm not just one for the road.

FREDDIE: No, no, I know, under normal circumstances, and so forth –

MOLLY: Under any circumstances. I have to be very careful –

FREDDIE: No, we are careful, of course we are – aren't you? Look here, Molly, I mean to say, look what I've been through –

MOLLY: You? You're flying, Freddie. You've ditched your woman there, left your children, stuffed your enemies – you're king of the castle.

FREDDIE: And you're my queen, my darling, my adorable Molly, queen of my heart, empress of the bedchamber.

MOLLY: You treat me like a chamber pot.

FREDDIE: Humbug! I treat you – look, I mean they'll be here any
             minute, come on, we can do this, I really want to, you
             know, I love you very much / and so on –

MOLLY: Get off me, you great lump –

FREDDIE: Lump? I'm half my weight because of your blasted
             eating habits, I'm hungry –

Freddie's phone rings.

FREDDIE   look, there they are –

MOLLY: Tell them to wait.

FREDDIE: I can't, there's a plane –

MOLLY: Tell them you're busy –

FREDDIE: Security bods –

MOLLY: – negotiating –

FREDDIE: – men on / motorbikes –

MOLLY: – with me. You matter to me Freddie. I know I'm just
             a young Irish lass, and you'll throw me to the wolves
             when / you're finished with –

FREDDIE: Never Molly, you're mine forever –

Freddie's phone rings.

MOLLY: But not now, is it? Not yet. I've got to wait, looking pretty and modest, standing at the window while you boom in parliament –

FREDDIE: Now look, they're waiting –

MOLLY: I want you Freddie, my body's crying out for you –

Bang on the door.

MOLLY: I want you –

FREDDIE: Oh Christ, no, look, I tell you what –

MOLLY: I want you now –

FREDDIE: Come in the car with me –

VOICE *(off)*: Prime Minister.

FREDDIE: *(shouts)* I'm coming. *(whispers)* Come with me. *(shouts)* Coming.

MOLLY: You don't love me.

FREDDIE: *(shouts)* Of course I love you.

VOICE *(off, louder)*: Prime Minister.

MOLLY: Go and be brave. Come back to me soon.

FREDDIE: God, Molly, I mean to say, you're marvellous –

VOICE *(off)*: Time's up, Prime Minister.

FREDDIE: *(shouts)* Yes, yes, wings of Hermes.
            Let me kiss you –

Banging on the door.

MOLLY: No Freddie, go and do your duty.

FREDDIE: Dammit! Dammit!

MOLLY stretches towards him.

FREDDIE: Dammit!

Freddie goes.

Music.

Act 1, Scene 2

*Following day, late afternoon. The Cabinet Office. A window, centre,
looks onto Whitehall. Drop-down bed in previous scene is now up,
appearing to be bookshelves, to one side of window. Table to other side.
Suggestion of sideboard and cupboards. Door on both sides of stage.*

FREDDIE seated. SERENA stands.

FREDDIE: Look, Serena, I need you to dial down the fuss when I
move about.

SERENA: We're protecting you, Prime Minister.

FREDDIE: Yes, yes, but every now and then I have to – ah, you
know – just toddle off on my bike without anyone /
noticing me –

SERENA: To see the Irish woman.

FREDDIE: She's very bright, you know.

SERENA: It's unwise, Prime Minister, we're not keen on her.

FREDDIE: Sharp. PR. Much brighter than – shake up the press
office here, I can tell you.

SERENA: We don't advise that.

FREDDIE: New broom, throw out the quill pens, get tweeting –

SERENA: The Bastard does not advise she move in to number 10.

FREDDIE: Fuck the Bastard, she's my First Lady.

SERENA: Hardly, Prime Minister.

FREDDIE: I need her by my side.

SERENA: Not a good look, Prime Minister – smacks of shaky foundations.

FREDDIE: What do you expect me to do, zip off on the back of a scooter like the little French chappie?

SERENA: You could stand by your wife.

FREDDIE: Listen, Serena, I mean, come on –

SERENA: Dame Serena, if you would, Prime Minister, this is a formal discussion.

FREDDIE: Oh for God's sake, I didn't slither up the greasy pole to be lectured by MI5 on the virtues of marriage. I remember when you were a very lively young filly cantering / about the west country –

SERENA: Prime Minister, we're here to discuss security arrangements. Tearing us out of Europe has left us scrabbling outside the most sophisticated security tent in the world. Largely constructed by us. It's a bloody nuisance.

FREDDIE: Look, I know, but buccaneering off was the only way I could elbow the girly-swot out of the way. Profile up massively.

SERENA: Well you've got your way, now grow up and see sense. We're all bored to death with this 'global Britain' tarradiddle.

FREDDIE: I know Serena, but you see, the thing is, now I'm – ah - a bit stuck with it.

SERENA: Oh come on, Freddie, you're PM now you can do what you like. You've got everyone hopping mad. Change your mind and they'll all be on the wrong foot.

FREDDIE: Molly wouldn't like it.

SERENA: So what, she's your floozy, not your future.

FREDDIE: No, look, she's very bright, surprisingly well educated –

SERENA: She's not even your type. You like your women with bigger hips, more to get hold of –

FREDDIE: That's not –

SERENA: – like that strapping girl who had one of your children. I thought you might have run with her for a bit.

FREDDIE: Well that was all a bit of a muddle, rather difficult moment, you know, not what I intended –

SERENA: Our country, Prime Minister, does not need someone who gets into a muddle. Your party, such as it is, does not need you to get it further into a muddle. MI5 certainly does not need you in a muddle. So listen to me –

FREDDIE: No, Serena, I will not listen you. I'm Prime Minister, numero uno, with a huge mandate to lead the Conservative Party to deliver on the instructions of the British people. So you / listen to me –

SERENA: Oh what nonsense, / there is no –

FREDDIE: We are going to free this country from the cloying /
              grip of the Establishment –

SERENA: Freddie, you're being / ridiculous –

FREDDIE: You're old hat / Serena, it's a new –

SERENA: I can't believe / I'm hearing this –

FREDDIE: I'm leading this brilliant, vigorous nation onwards to
              new heights, back to its roots, sunlit uplands –

SERENA: Freddie, shut up.

FREDDIE: I won't –

SERENA: Shut up.

FREDDIE: It's different –

SERENA: It's the same. Your friends are my friends. We've done
              well, Freddie, but I grew up faster than you because I'm
              a woman. Catch up. You can do better – much, much
              better.

FREDDIE: I think I've done / all right –

SERENA: There's an unmarked car outside the back door, ready
              to drive you to Molly's. You must have the security
              bod in case some of her Irish chums want to settle old
              scores. Go and let her give you a good time, little Miss
              No-hips. You can always change your mind.

FREDDIE: I –

SERENA: Go on. Prime Minister.

FREDDIE goes.

Music.

Act 1, Scene 3

Following day, early afternoon. MOLLY's flat. MOLLY is dressing.
SEAN appears outside the window.

SEAN: Ulster says no.

MOLLY: I said no.

SEAN: You were about to say yes.

MOLLY: That was deliberate.

SEAN climbs in through the window.

SEAN: I heard you. You were falling into the arms of the
            British Establishment. You'd better be very careful.

MOLLY: So everyone tells me.

SEAN: Listen to me. You're doing well. You're driving
            Branscombe mad. But you're forgetting Ulster.

MOLLY: Don't you dare say that. My father was shot dead, three
            bullets, in front of my eyes in our hallway. I was eight.
            They would have shot me too –

SEAN: No, no, I know, Molly. I know.

MOLLY: I'm doing our work here. I don't need you on my back.
            Just keep paying the rent.

SEAN: When are you moving into Downing Street there?

MOLLY: When the time's right.

SEAN: We've got money for one more month here.

MOLLY: Well, find some more. I'll need more clothes, new shoes.

SEAN: We gave you money for a dress –

MOLLY: For here, that was for here. We're moving into Downing
            Street.

SEAN: You can wear the dress there –

MOLLY: I'm First Lady of the United Kingdom, I can't wear that.

SEAN: Your Mam's thrilled. I saw her sister the other day
            and she said your Mam couldn't hardly believe it, her
            little Molly, used to be the little devil, she was, up to all
            sorts of no good, marrying herself to a British Prime
            Minister.

MOLLY: I'm putting myself in danger for Ulster. I need the
            shoes.

SEAN: Money's very tight. You're putting something by from
            your day-job?

MOLLY: Tell those idiot Stormont deputies to get off their pudgy
            arses and knock on doors.

SEAN: All right, Molly, quieten down –

MOLLY: I will not quiet down, so I won't, I've spent a lot of my
            free time seducing Freddie Branscombe and I'm not
            properly respected by the Unionist community.

MOLLY *(cont)*:   Tell them I'll stop the customs border carving a line in blood through the Irish Sea when I see an increase in my pay and a very substantial clothes allowance. I'm moving to Downing Street.

SEAN: I don't think I can / get them to –

MOLLY: And not before, do you hear me? If your brother wants to carry on selling his onions to Liverpool without going through the customs I need money for new shoes.

Music.

Act 1, Scene 4

Following day, lunchtime. MOLLY's flat. MOLLY is dressing. FREDDIE comes, flustered.

FREDDIE: Molly, thank God, take me in your arms. I've had no lunch. Do we have any of that decent red left?

MOLLY: My great Freddie-teddy, sit yourself down, will you, take the weight off your feet.

FREDDIE: Enough about weight.

MOLLY: I like something to get hold of.

FREDDIE: You're bloody marvellous, Molly, I don't know what I would do –

MOLLY: You'd find someone else.

FREDDIE: No, Molly, no I wouldn't not now, not –

MOLLY: Women can't resist you. You've funny hair, more energy than four boys half your age – and you're king of the castle.

FREDDIE: I don't know Molly, I mean, you know, greasy pole and all that, I mean is this the top? You're the tops.

MOLLY: I am. Don't you forget it.

FREDDIE: Did you say there's some red?

MOLLY: Sit back in your chair.

MOLLY straddles FREDDIE as he sits.

MOLLY: This tie comes off, for one.

FREDDIE: If I had a drink –

MOLLY undoes her blouse.

MOLLY: And this for two –

FREDDIE: Have a drink anytime.

MOLLY: Any time.

MOLLY slides off her blouse.

MOLLY: Any time. What you said to that American woman, wasn't it?

FREDDIE: Her? Business arrangement, all over –

MOLLY: I'll come round any time, was it?

FREDDIE: Look ages ago, I mean, nothing –

MOLLY: How do you think I feel about it?

FREDDIE: There's nothing to feel.

MOLLY leans over FREDDIE.

MOLLY: Is that right?

FREDDIE: Oh my God Molly you're so –

MOLLY: Downing Street.

FREDDIE: Molly let me undo –

MOLLY: We're moving into Downing Street.

FREDDIE: Yes, of course, my gorgeous little –

MOLLY: Now.

FREDDIE: Yes, look, as soon as –

MOLLY: Moving in now.

FREDDIE: We're somewhat in medias res, just at this –

MOLLY: All the photos are just me coming out of this dingy
            front door. I need to come out of 10 Downing Street,
            Freddie. Into the flashlights.

FREDDIE: No, look, very soon –

MOLLY presses herself on FREDDIE and bounces, slowly then faster.

MOLLY: Now, Freddie. Now. Now. Now. Now.

FREDDIE: Oh. Oh, Molly.

MOLLY quickly gets off him.

MOLLY: I spoke to Sergey Susemihl today.

FREDDIE: I need a drink. Is there a drink?

MOLLY: I spoke to him just there.

FREDDIE: Susemihl? He's long gone.

MOLLY: He sends you a message. Greetings from Moscow.

FREDDIE: On the phone? To you?

MOLLY: He wants to get the old Conservative Friends of Russia
             gang together again.

FREDDIE: Why did he call –

MOLLY: I was at the same party as you. You didn't know me
             then.

FREDDIE: Of course I did, I've always known you –

MOLLY: You were too busy funding the American woman.

FREDDIE: Oh, shut up about her Molly.

MOLLY: Shut up, is it?

FREDDIE: No, no, I didn't mean – what else did he say?

MOLLY: Is it speak up, or shut up, Freddie?

FREDDIE: What did he say? I can't talk to Susemihl, the spooks
             would go mad.

MOLLY: I'll talk to him for you.

FREDDIE: No, God no, complete stroganoff – did you give him
             your number?

MOLLY: He couldn't get through to you.

FREDDIE: Look, stay out of it, stay away from him for God's sake, you'll screw up everything –

MOLLY: Oh is it? Stay behind the curtains, smile at the back of the photo. Like my country, is it, have a billion pounds, now keep quiet? I'm telling you, Freddie, Ulster is not quiet, and won't be till you –

FREDDIE: Oh, now come on, my turtledove, you sound like Diana the huntress setting her dogs –

MOLLY: You're tearing my country out of our United Kingdom, throwing us to the nationalist wolves. Six months ago you were sniffing around my skirt, wife threw you out you said, take me in you said. I said what about Ulster? Engraved on my heart, you said.

FREDDIE: Look, no-one will notice the difference, it'll be seamless and when this free trade thing – I promise you, it'll – I didn't know you felt so –

MOLLY: You don't know. That's what I'm here to tell you.

FREDDIE: I thought –

MOLLY: You don't think.

            Do you want to touch my body?

FREDDIE: What – is the Pope –

MOLLY: Don't tell me about the Pope! Tear up your rotten deal with the Fenians and lie down on the bed.

Music.

Act 2, Scene 1

Following day, mid-morning. MOLLY's flat. MOLLY is dressing. SEAN comes in through the window

SEAN: There it is, the money for you.

MOLLY: I'm to be moving to Downing Street the next week. You'll get a rebate from the landlord here, you can add that to it.

SEAN: No, that's DUP funds. I'll need to credit that back to the central account.

MOLLY: The party's overflowing like Dunseverick Falls. You've not spent half the money you got from Theresa May. The rebate comes to me, Sean.

SEAN: I don't know, Molly -

MOLLY: Listen, I've seduced the British Prime Minister as instructed. I've not had my bonus. You're keeping me on low-grade wages. Our so-called politicians have rolled over in front of Freddie Branscombe.

SEAN: Just like you, Molly.

MOLLY: For my country! They're building their mansions, buying their farms while they sell Ulster down the river. I'm on my own, betrayed by my people, betrayed by my country.

SEAN: There it is, I tell you, I've brought you more money.

MOLLY: How much?

SEAN: Fifty-five pounds, eighty pence.

MOLLY: You're out of your depth! Ten grubby five-pound notes
            wouldn't buy the zip of the dress I need.

SEAN: That's eleven, there.

MOLLY: You get back there and tell them, Sean Smallwood, tell
            them I'm worth more money than they can think of.
            Tell them I want a new manager.

SEAN: I've known you since you were a wee one.

MOLLY: We're not round the back lanes of Garvagh any more.
            I'm fighting for Ulster, I'm fighting for my Da, I'm at
            the top of the tree, Sean, I need professionals around
            me not errand boys.

SEAN: No Molly, now that's harsh, I've looked after you, your
            Mam trusts me / to make sure you don't –

FREDDIE comes.

FREDDIE: Molly, listen, I've just got a few moments before you get
            dressed – who's this?

MOLLY: My dressmaker.

FREDDIE: Looks like an errand boy. What's he doing here at this
            time of the morning?

MOLLY: It's eleven o'clock.

FREDDIE: Why aren't you dressed?

MOLLY: I thought you might drop in.

FREDDIE: Sweetheart, look, I've not got long – *(to SEAN)* have you delivered it?

MOLLY: He's my dressmaker, for when we move in to Downing Street. I want to look beautiful for you.

FREDDIE: You look marvellous, darling. *(To SEAN)* Would you mind giving us a few moments?

MOLLY: He's come to talk about samples.

FREDDIE: Samples of what? Are you pregnant?

MOLLY: Fabrics, Freddie.

SEAN: Cotton, wool –

MOLLY: Not cotton, 'Albert' *(in French accent)*.

FREDDIE: Ah, I say, Albert, ah, Albert –

SEAN: *(French accent)* Lefèvre. Albert Lefèvre.

FREDDIE: M. Lefèvre, fine Parisian couture and so forth –

MOLLY: They're in Shoreditch.

SEAN: We have a small 'atelier' in Shoreditch, women's clothing, bed-linen, fancy goods, everything for the newly-weds.

MOLLY: That's not us.

SEAN: Your maman, she know it is only a small matter of
              time.

Knock on the door.

FREDDIE: Oh Christ, tempus fugit.

SEAN: Tempora mutantur et nos mutamur in illis, monsieur.

FREDDIE: I say, that's rather à propos, you know.

VOICE *(off)*: Prime Minister.

SEAN: It is an humble honour to meet you, sir. Perhaps you
              would care to visit our petit atelier. Young brides
              are enchanting to choose the new materials, soft
              furnishing, romantic hanging for the marital chambre –

VOICE *(off)*: Sorry to interrupt, Prime Minister.

FREDDIE: M. Lefèvre, I'm being hounded by these chappies.
              Molly, the misery of it is –

SEAN: You must dash, monsieur –

FREDDIE: Spot on, M. Lefèvre.

MOLLY: Will you leave me so soon?

FREDDIE: Look, Molly –

VOICE *(off)*: Prime Minister.

MOLLY: No, you must go –

FREDDIE: Molly, dammit – M. Lefèvre, come and see me would
              you? –

MOLLY: I'm not important –

VOICE *(off)*: Sir, we have / to move –

FREDDIE: M. Lefèvre will – won't you – dammit, I have to –
              Molly –

FREDDIE goes in haste.

MOLLY: You idiot, what was all that nonsense about the 'atelier'
              and talking in Latin?

SEAN: You needed cover. And you didn't tell me he was
              coming. That's very dangerous for me, Molly. I'd say
              that's a disciplinary, I'll have to talk to the party, no
              surprises, you know, it's not good at all.

MOLLY: Get out of my house.

SEAN: It's only a wee flat.

MOLLY: Out! I'm going to be on to your superior.

SEAN: You don't know who that is.

MOLLY: I'll get it out of you soon enough.

SEAN: I don't know who it is.

MOLLY: Sergey Susemihl might be able to tell you, no?

SEAN: Susemihl? Who's – ? Jesus, Mary and Joseph!

SEAN flees through the window.

MOLLY: *(spotlit, to audience)* Jesus, Mary and Joseph – where
               were they when the IRA shot my Da? They knock on
               the door, my Da opens it and Bang! and shouts and
               Bang! Bang! and the crash of my Da to the floor and
               me stood there in my little orange dress holding my
               spoon for breakfast.

Act 2, Scene 2

*Following day, breakfast. The Cabinet Office. FREDDIE at the
table, reading the Daily Telegraph, eating croissants. SEAN comes,
flamboyant.*

FREDDIE: M. Lefèvre, bonjour my friend, bonjour, how very kind,
trop gentil –

SEAN: Mais non, monsieur, c'est à moi, c'est tout à moi le
plaisir.

FREDDIE: Yes, yes, very good, now then, look the thing is I
thought you were, ah –

SEAN: Errand boy. Ha! It's very funny, M. le premier ministre,
I, an artiste –

FREDDIE: The thing is, Molly used you very badly, but it just
wasn't fair, I turned up all of a sudden, I mean, between
you and me, M. Lefèvre –

SEAN: Albert, please monsieur, -

FREDDIE: I say, Albert, that's – well the thing of it is Molly's very
highly strung of course – well, you'll know, she's your
client, you'll have her measurements and so forth.

SEAN: A very beautiful woman, Mademoiselle McCloy.

FREDDIE: Do you think so? Some of my friends think she's plain.

SEAN: *(aside, Irish accent)* They've not met her mother.

FREDDIE: What?

SEAN: *(French accent)* Mon Dieu! Look out for her brother. A giant of a man.

FREDDIE: I didn't know she had a brother.

SEAN: Three. Six. All giants.

FREDDIE: Well, ah – look, Albert, I need your help. I want you to make a dress.

SEAN: Ah, the wedding dress.

FREDDIE: No, an evening dress.

SEAN: For the reception. Molly's mother will be beside herself there with joy.

FREDDIE: Look, you're right, I know we need to get this wedding business over the line and move on and we will, I assure you. No, the dress is for the Irish.

SEAN: The Irish do not understand couture.

FREDDIE: Albert, old man, I know, plain to see, but I want Molly to shine, she is my star, my guiding light, my –

SEAN: Monsieur is the great lover.

FREDDIE: You have it Albert! She must feel my love in your satin, your silks, the artistry of your cut, your stitch.

SEAN: The Irish are not easy.

FREDDIE: I'll pay double your asking price. I must have it. Albert, you don't know how critical –

SERENA comes.

SERENA: Prime Minister, who is this?

FREDDIE: This? He's – ah –

SERENA: The meeting with the French begins in four minutes. Who is this?

FREDDIE: Well, look here, Serena -

SERENA: Who, Prime Minister?

FREDDIE: Ah – well, now, Dame Serena Ridinghard, let me introduce M. Albert Lefèvre.

SERENA: Bonjour monsieur, you are one of the French delegation?

SEAN: Mais oui, your majesty, je suis enchanté –

FREDDIE: He's a dressmaker.

SERENA: There are no dressmakers in the French delegation.

FREDDIE: No, no, he's from Shoreditch.

SERENA: Prime Minister, my assistant has your briefing notes for the meeting. 'M. Lefèvre' will no doubt excuse you, as you make your way downstairs.

FREDDIE: We haven't finished –

SERENA: Won't you, M. Lefèvre?

FREDDIE: All right, all right, look, Albert, we'll carry on – you
             must excuse –

FREDDIE goes.

SERENA: Stand away from the window.

             Smallwood, where are we?

SEAN: *(Irish accent)* 10 Downing Street.

SERENA: And who am I, Smallwood?

SEAN: Dame Ridinghard –

SERENA: Who am I?

SEAN: N.

SERENA: Correct. N. And you are?

SEAN: Special Operative Smallwood, N.

SERENA: How many ranks are there between us?

SEAN: Nine, N.

SERENA: Eleven. And where's your beat?

SEAN: Wandsworth, N.

SERENA: Whilst I might note your tradecraft in getting into
              Downing Street, why in God's name are you a French
              tailor?

SEAN: Couturier, it's very different, do you see –

SERENA: Thank you Smallwood. Your job is to keep Molly on
              a tight leash, not to tempt Branscombe into a fashion
              frenzy. God knows which Treasury trough he'll slurp to
              decorate little Miss No-hips.

SEAN: Albert Lefèvre was Molly's idea.

SERENA: You're running Molly, not the other way round. I was
              never impressed by you, but, I'm loath to say it, you've
              kept her on track. She's got Freddie by the balls, she's
              been frumpy in the background, now starting to do
              the silly little royal wave. This is promotable work
              Smallwood. Get back to Wandsworth. Do the work and
              don't screw it up.

SEAN goes.

Music.

Act 2, Scene 3

*Following night, small hours. MOLLY's flat. FREDDIE in bed. MOLLY,
spotlit, standing in dark red negligée, gazing front.*

*Music, same track continuing from end of previous scene very quietly
beneath MOLLY's speech until MOLLY turns up the music.*

MOLLY: I was fifteen. I knew I was a looker. I went to Portrush
on the bus with this boy Enda, Sean Smallwood's
second cousin or something, just as stupid, he said
come to Lush, there's so many people, the music's a
power, there's hell's crush. Mam didn't know we'd gone.
There was E and stuff, a mass of people, Enda said,
here's one, take it, it's wild, and the sound's so heavy
and I'm dancing, arms all up and waving and there's
this beauty of a boy eyeing me and he's close and he
yells in my ear, PATRICK. DERRY. I yell, GARVAGH.
He smiles. YOU A PRODDY? Must get out, get away,
squeeze past him but he holds on to me and I scream
and no-one can hear me the music banging so loud.

MOLLY turns up the music.

FREDDIE: What the fuck is that? Molly turn it off, what the hell…
come back to bed, what are you doing?

Molly turns off music with remote.

MOLLY: Nothing.

FREDDIE: Come back. It's pitch dark. Have a cuddle.

MOLLY: Not now.

FREDDIE: Come on, look, what's the time, you can sleep after they
              pick me up.

MOLLY: I'm tired of waiting.

FREDDIE: Then come back to bed. Cuddle'll do you good. Not
              long now.

MOLLY: When? When are we moving in?

FREDDIE: Few things to sort out.

MOLLY: Do you love your country?

FREDDIE: Not now darling, I must –

MOLLY: Where will you be laid to rest?

FREDDIE: *(sleepy)* Look, I don't know, somewhere.

MOLLY: The sleep of heaven.

FREDDIE: Here and now would be marvellous Molly, come and
              be quiet.

MOLLY: I fled from my church. Your man suffocated our
              loss. I'm here telling you Freddie, I'm fighting for my
              country, d'you hear me?

FREDDIE: *(muffled)* Lie down.

MOLLY: Do you love your country?

FREDDIE: Yes, if you'll lie down and / go to sleep –

MOLLY: And is it my country?

FREDDIE: *(roused)* No it's my country, I'm the Prime Minister and
            if you don't shut up I'll throw you out. Lie down.

MOLLY: Our God has an Armalite leaning against his throne.
            We serve him in the pure way, before Catholics ever
            came to Ireland. Did you know that, Freddie? They
            bled our land for a thousand years but we will not be
            defeated. You'll be true to us, Freddie, won't you there,
            and keep Ulster close to your heart? Freddie. Freddie?
            Do you hear me there, Freddie?

FREDDIE   *(muffled again)* What?

MOLLY: I'm saying our mission here. I'm going forward,
            Freddie, are you with me?

FREDDIE: *(into the pillow)* Other way round, old thing.

MOLLY: Old thing! I'm not your woman's bedsocks. Look!

MOLLY pulls her top tight at the waist.

            Look, Freddie-teddy, is this your old thing? Are you
            with me? Do you want to come with me?

FREDDIE: *(rousing)* Molly, come here, I can't see you properly.

MOLLY: Do you want to look, is it? Do you want other people to
            look? Look at you with me by your side?

FREDDIE: Come here, for Christ's sake.

MOLLY stands over him by the bedside. FREDDIE struggles to touch her.

MOLLY: Tell me when.

MOLLY bends towards him.

FREDDIE: You know I need you in Downing Street.

MOLLY: Now.

FREDDIE: Yes, yes, now of course, week or two at the most, come here.

MOLLY: Too long.

FREDDIE: Look, it's tricky, Cabinet re-shuffle coming up, all sorts of people coming and going.

MOLLY: Reshuffle, is it?

MOLLY leans close over FREDDIE.

MOLLY: Keep me out of the way while you play with your toys?

FREDDIE: Molly, lie down, God's sake, you're –

MOLLY: I'm yours, Freddie, yours for the taking. What do you like best? Do you want me, Freddie?

FREDDIE: Molly, get into bed, I can't wait any longer –

MOLLY: Neither can I. This week –

FREDDIE: Molly!

MOLLY: Latest. Downing Street.

FREDDIE: I don't, I mean – the Bastard – I'll have to speak to –

MOLLY: You're the fucking Prime Minister. Tell him. Tell him I'm coming this week. Pull off the sheet and let me see you standing proud –

FREDDIE: This week, Molly, I'm – Molly -

MOLLY: I'm going to ride you, you great white submarine, hand over the joystick, Captain Branscombe –

FREDDIE: Stop, stop Molly –

MOLLY: We're moving in, Freddie -

FREDDIE: No, no, stop –

MOLLY: Waving from the front door -

FREDDIE: No, Molly, oh – oh – oh!

MOLLY: Oh. You've fired your missile, Cap'n Branscombe. Gone off too soon, is it? Missed the target. What a waste of public money.

FREDDIE: Oh Christ, Molly –

MOLLY: That's no good, Freddie, is it?

MOLLY draws away and sits on the end of the bed facing away from FREDDIE.

MOLLY: You'll have to practise. Otherwise when you ask me to
             marry you, I might have to think about it.

FREDDIE: Marry?

MOLLY turns on the music with a remote.

FREDDIE: No, Molly, I've got to sleep.

MOLLY: You'll tell them. First thing. *(She yells in his ear)* End of
             the week!

Music.

Act 2, Scene 4

Following night, midnight. MOLLY's flat. MOLLY is in fashionable shapewear, doing yoga exercises. SEAN climbs in through the window. MOLLY continues her yoga during the first section of the dialogue.

SEAN: Where's Branscombe?

MOLLY: The Bastard told him to chair a meeting about flood defences.

SEAN: Is he coming back?

MOLLY: He doesn't care about floods.

SEAN: We'd better be quick. You've not put in your expenses.

MOLLY: I'm busy.

SEAN: The DUP are worried. Your last claim didn't match up to the cash you've spent. Some had VAT, some not. Your claim's a muddle.

MOLLY: I'm fighting for our lives.

SEAN: The party's running short. You see, there's not the subscriptions now.

MOLLY: I have him tight by the balls there. I'm moving in.

SEAN: I've to ask you to get your paperwork tidy, because – well – you see, the Treasurer's got an inspector from HMRC coming in –

MOLLY springs up from her yoga position.

MOLLY: I don't do VAT. The British are shafting our people, you tell them, I'm doing my job. I'll be in Downing Street this week, you'll see the picture of me coming out the front door. The world will see it, isn't it? And I'll be crying out for Ulster.

SEAN: No, you're doing a wonderful job Molly, of course you are. I tell them that, I do. The thing is –

MOLLY: The DUP lost seats, the stupid idiots, no hold over the Tories now, isn't it? I'm their only hope. My fingers tight round the Prime Minister's lever of power.

SEAN: I don't know your Mam would like to hear that now Molly.

MOLLY: My Mam hears the gunshots in her head every morning as the sun shines in our front door. Your people should hear them. Tell them not to forget.

SEAN: No, Molly, they don't forget. Look, there's been a meeting high up in the DUP.

MOLLY: There is no high up in the DUP.

SEAN: They've made a decision, just now, isn't it –

MOLLY: Stunted short-arses –

SEAN: and what they've decided there – / to tell you the truth –

MOLLY: scrabbling for scraps –

SEAN: You see, the thing of it is now, now that Stormont and all – what they're saying is – they'll be shutting down the mission.

MOLLY: Which mission?

SEAN: This one, now.

MOLLY: My mission?

SEAN: It's the most expensive.

MOLLY: I'm costing nothing.

SEAN: Well, you know, what with the shoes and the clothes – Albert Lefèvre, you know –

MOLLY: What do they think it's costing me? You told me I would be civil service. That's too old and slow, this is the only way now to stop them selling Ulster to the Papists.

SEAN: Ah, well, Molly, we're maybe too quick –

MOLLY: Who's telling you this?

SEAN: You know, with the HMRC it is, coming in –

MOLLY: Is it MI5 looking over their shoulder?

SEAN: You know how they talk.

MOLLY: Who talks? Have you talked? Bossy Ridinghard, has she got on to you, Sean?

SEAN: I don't know her at all.

MOLLY: Are you a leaker? You're a marked man, Sean
               Smallwood, you know. We're doing God's work here.
               Some Free Presbyterian elders will stoke the fires of hell
               under your arse, you know that.

SEAN: I know, I know Molly, you mustn't stir them up now,
               will you? I'm the one looking after you.

MOLLY: Does the Bastard know who I am?

SEAN: Ridinghard hates him, he won't know.

MOLLY: You're Ridinghard's donkey.

SEAN: No!

MOLLY: She's whipping your back.

SEAN: No, No Molly, I report to Belfast, only Belfast. I don't
               know her at all. Never met her. And to your auntie,
               of course, to your dear grandmother's sister. Do you
               remember when you / were a wee one –

MOLLY: Change their minds, or I'm telling my people in the
               church. It'll be concrete shoes into the Lagan for you,
               Sean.

SEAN: You wouldn't do that.

MOLLY: I'm done with you, I'm too far above you now, I'm
               telling you –

FREDDIE comes.

FREDDIE: Bloody north! Don't get this flooding nonsense in Oxfordshire. M. Lefèvre, how nice to see you. Working late. Molly, get us a nightcap, would you, darling, I'm absolutely whackers.

SEAN: Ah! Mister le, premier – minister –

MOLLY: Mr Lefèvre is just leaving.

FREDDIE: Nonsense, working all hours, he needs a drink, we all do –

MOLLY: He's not working for us, now.

FREDDIE: Oh come now, Molly, we don't toss over old friends like that. What'll it be Albert, drop of whisky, or I think we've got some rather drinkable claret, have we, darling?

SEAN: Monsieur is very kind – but the devil's buttermilk is the drink there -

MOLLY: He's out, I tell you. His designs don't suit me.

FREDDIE: Oh they will, my huntress. I'm not saying anything, but Albert and I may have a little surprise for a special moment for a very special little woman. What, Albert?

SEAN: Under la table, monsieur, say nothing!

FREDDIE: Ah yes! Right, old man. Molly, all will be well.

MOLLY: I'm after telling you, isn't it – Mr Lefèvre is leaving this house.

FREDDIE: Just open the bottle, sweetheart. I'm worn out. Do you
            know, Albert, I've spent the day marching my socks
            off up and down our marvellous red wall like bloody
            Hadrian. Back to London, sit down to dinner with
            some old Buller chums, the Bastard throws them out,
            has me and the night staff down to the bunker banging
            on about floods.

MOLLY: Sack him.

FREDDIE: Not on, old girl.

MOLLY: Freddie, darling, the '16 or the '17, is it?

MOLLY beckons FREDDIE to the drinks cabinet at the side of the stage.
She winds herself around him.

MOLLY: I was sixteen once, Freddie. Sweet sixteen. I was a
            looker then. My skin was like silk. I smelled of the
            breeze-blown grass of the fields of Ireland –

SEAN makes his escape through the window.

MOLLY: – and the softer, darker places of my body, Freddie,
            were the secret wooded clefts in the hills. Are you
            weary and worn, Freddie boy, will I take you to my soft
            Irish bed?

FREDDIE: Well now, look – M. Lefèvre is still – where is he?

MOLLY: It's just us, my sweet king of the world.

FREDDIE: I say. He's very polite. Continental.

MOLLY: Take a shower. I'll turn down the bed.

FREDDIE: My god, I mean hit the jackpot, what? PM, huge
             majority, gorgeous woman, glass of wine –

MOLLY: Soap, shower and towel yourself up and come back to
             me as Lug Lámfota, come back and search deep inside
             me, deep, deep and find my jackpot. Will you do that
             for me, is it?

FREDDIE: By Jove, Molly, come here –

MOLLY: Shower, Freddie.

FREDDIE: I've known you for ever –

MOLLY: Susemihl's party, it was.

FREDDIE: Don't need him now –

MOLLY: Shower. This jackpot's a rollover, I promise you.

FREDDIE: Wings of –

MOLLY: Hermes. I know. Go.

Freddie goes.

Music.

MOLLY: He was funny, Sergey Susemihl. A grown-up spy. I
             don't know. He was like a beaver. He beavered up to
             me at the bar in the Archangel club, started on about
             Archangel in Russia, then Archangel Michael then
             I looked like an angel I told him about the fields of
             Ulster and he bought us another drink.

Music stops.

MOLLY: All whiskery, like a beaver. Quite soft. Said to call
              him, if ever I needed anything. I said did he trust the
              English? If I wanted to see Moscow he would show me
              around. Bought us another drink.

FREDDIE comes, a towel around his waist.

FREDDIE: Tomorrow, my gazelle, tomorrow as ever is I want you
              in Downing Street.

MOLLY: Freddie!

FREDDIE: I told the Bastard.

MOLLY: You're a manly man.

FREDDIE: The bed's old but it's bloody huge. Tonight, for the last
              time in our sweet love-nest, I shall be your swan-like
              Jove, you my Leda.

Music.

Act 2 Scene 5

Same night. Midnight. The Cabinet Office. SEAN seated. SERENA standing in the shadows, only her face is sharply lit from the side, noirish.

SERENA: We're bringing her in. Tell me everything.

SEAN: Well, N, you see Molly's great-auntie was my grandmother's half-sister, on my father's side that is, do you know, she was a very sweet old thing, dear to everyone, she had a little farm up the road, away in the back of Caheny, over there by the river Bann and I just remember –

SERENA: Tell me everything important.

SEAN: You know N, isn't it, it's important to grasp the deep background as they say in the business.

SERENA: I am the business, Smallwood.

SEAN: Yes N, of course that's it. Well, Molly's father was shot –

SERENA: I know that, tell me the background –

SEAN: Well the farm was mainly dairy –

SERENA: Not the deep background you idiot –

SEAN: Is it the near background, N, that I'm telling you? With a little bit of foreground?

SERENA: Is she vulnerable?

SEAN: She's always asking for money.

SERENA: The DUP pays her.

SEAN: Well they don't pay us so much, N. I'm after asking
             them myself for a bit of a loan every now and then –

SERENA: We gave the DUP a billion pounds. You were supposed
             to spend it before we set Stormont going again.

SEAN: Not me, N!

SERENA: Your people. It's like dealing with the seven dwarves. The
             Bastard can't wait for you to give up and join the south.

SEAN: Never, N. Ulster says no.

SERENA: So we hear. It's like an ear-worm.

             You tell me Molly's a fanatic.

SEAN: She is that, N. That's why we groomed her for the
             mission.

SERENA: There were other fathers murdered.

SEAN: She was just a wee one.

SERENA: What else?

SEAN: The church, N. Her family are strong in the
             Presbyterians, but boys drew her towards the Frees.

SERENA: What did she need from them?

SEAN: They were after killing back.

SERENA: Did she kill?

SEAN   Well now, I'm not so sure –

SERENA: You're paid to be sure. Did she kill?

SEAN: She may have sat in the back of the car. I stopped her
            from going down that road –

SERENA: Why?

SEAN: Her Mam wouldn't like it.

SERENA: She'd left home.

SEAN: Well, I was her home, you see, in Belfast.

SERENA: Are you the weak link? What else wouldn't her Mam like?

SEAN: Her Mam's a quiet one.

SERENA: A good woman?

SEAN: She didn't like the noise.

SERENA: The gunshots.

SEAN: The music. Molly was into the dancing. With the boys.
            I couldn't stop her from that.

SERENA: Why would you?

SEAN: They took her into the Frees, Ulster Resistance –

SERENA: Your thugs.

SEAN: They're not my people!

SERENA: She wanted to kill.

SEAN: She was taken by the music. The boys –

SERENA: The sex.

SEAN: I don't know.

SERENA: Does she enjoy it? Is that what drives her?

SEAN: She wants to save our country from the Fenians.

SERENA: She might forget Ulster and just bathe in the limelight.
             Sex may be her weakness.

SEAN: She'd never do that.

SERENA: We have to keep her on track.

SEAN: I'm looking after her. I said to her mam –

SERENA: You're in over your pay-grade, Smallwood. I shall find
             her out. Tomorrow we'll endure your pantomime tailor
             for the last time, then Molly completes her mission.
             Alone.

SEAN: I told her Mam I would look after her.

SERENA: Molly will report to me.

Music.

<h1 style="text-align:center">Act 2 Scene 6</h1>

Following day, early evening. The Cabinet Office. MOLLY is wearing a demure floral print, with tones of orange. SERENA stands by the drinks cabinet.

SERENA: Sherry?

MOLLY: I will not be questioned.

SERENA: We can't recognise you until you've been vetted.

SERENA hands sherry to MOLLY.

MOLLY: I am mistress of Downing Street. I'll not be told what to do.

SERENA: You may be living in Downing Street, but you're not here, officially.

MOLLY: Ask the Prime Minister.

SERENA: He says you're long-term, not fly-by-night. So we have to vet you for security and he approved it.

MOLLY: He never did so.

SERENA: Of course he did, ducky. One of our gentleman callers will have a chat with you back at your little bed-sit.

MOLLY: I'm not answering anything there.

SERENA: Sweetheart, you're playing with the grown-ups now –

MOLLY: Don't call me –

SERENA: The Prime Minister is enthralled by your body, but
              we have the nation to run. Until we officially know all
              about you we can't have you ordering Downing Street
              curtains in provincial Irish prints. More sherry?

MOLLY: Keep your gnats' piss.

SERENA: Be in your flat at 0800 tomorrow. Our gentlemen will
              visit –

MOLLY: I will not so! Your job, Ridinghard, is in the gift of the
              Prime / Minister and I'll –

SERENA: Oh you do look fine when you're angry. You're very
              clever – simper in public; behind closed doors you're
              a tigress. I'm not sure Freddie knows quite what he's
              taken on –

MOLLY: I've taken him on. He loves me and we're to marry. He
              doesn't trust any of you. I give him what he needs to be
              a brilliant Prime Minister. He tells me everything –

SERENA: That's rather the problem, darling. If you were in full
              flow in my bed, I might tell you more than was strictly
              appropriate.

MOLLY: I wouldn't be found dead in your bed.

SERENA: What are your weaknesses, my sweet? Where's your
              soft underbelly?

MOLLY: You're too close –

SERENA: Where are your chinks, the secret cracks the enemy could pry open to soften you up, Molly? We have to keep you safe.

MOLLY: Don't touch me. Like that!

SERENA: You're safe with us, Molly. Answer our questions, they're very simple, and you'll have all the protection the state can give. So will your mother.

MOLLY: What about my mother?

SERENA: She's worried about you.

MOLLY: She's not.

SERENA: She thinks you've left her behind.

MOLLY: She does not. She's thrilled I'm to be married.

SERENA: Not to the Prime Minister who's betrayed her.

MOLLY: I'm keeping Ulster safe for her. You don't know what she feels.

SERENA: Smallwood told us.

MOLLY: Sean Smallwood's a leaker?

SERENA nods.

MOLLY: The slimy little toad that he is.

SERENA touches MOLLY'S arm.

MOLLY: I'll kill the snake. The elders of the Free Presbyterian church shall hear of this.

SERENA turns MOLLY to face the audience and lightly holds her round the waist from behind. MOLLY lit as Joan of Arc.

MOLLY: All Ulster shall hear of this. Throughout history betrayed and betrayed by our own. Carson was betrayed. Lloyd George betrayed us, but Ulster stood proud. 'British as Finchley' – Thatcher betrayed us. The English don't care about Ulster. I will make Freddie care.

SERENA holds MOLLY closely to her from behind, facing the front. FREDDIE and SEAN come.

SERENA: *(still facing front)* Prime Minister, Miss McCloy and I are taking sherry. M. Lefèvre might like the Bristol Cream.

FREDDIE: Yes, yes, of course. Is Molly all right?

SERENA: She's overcome by her sudden responsibilities as mistress of Downing Street.

FREDDIE: The curtains?

SEAN: Mademoiselle shall have no fears. Chez nous, in our little Shoreditch atelier, we have just the fabrics Mlle McCloy desires.

MOLLY: Your atelier!

FREDDIE: Marvellous, Albert, we'll come over tomorrow morning.

SERENA: US Secretary of State, Prime Minister.

FREDDIE: Oh god, really? Can't he come in the afternoon?
              Sweetheart, Albert and I have a little surprise for you.

MOLLY: A surprise, is it? The worm.

FREDDIE: No, Molly, look – look here – it's something very
              special to celebrate –

MOLLY: I'm going to grind the slug under my heel.

SEAN: Will mademoiselle stand over there, please, as we
              reveal la surprise.

SERENA: Come here by me.

MOLLY: Get off – Freddie get this creepy woman off me, can't
              you?

FREDDIE: Look what M. Lefèvre has created for you, my darling,
              to celebrate your arrival in Downing Street.

*SEAN unfolds a glittering, narrow-waisted evening dress in exquisitely
bias-cut green silk, diamonds clustered at the low-slung bodice.*

SEAN: Voilà, mademoiselle. I hope it please you well.

SERENA: No cost spared, I see, M. Lefèvre.

FREDDIE: Marvellous, Albert, old man. Molly, look, my darling,
              look, this is my gift to you. You will be by my side at the
              posh do for the American chappie and no-one will be
              looking at him.

MOLLY: The colour –

FREDDIE: You'll look wonderful –

MOLLY: The colour –

SEAN: It will set off mademoiselle's pale neck of a swan –

MOLLY: The colour –

SERENA: It matches your eyes, dear –

MOLLY: It's Fenian green!

MOLLY grabs the bottle of Bristol Cream.

FREDDIE: The Bastard said anything but orange.

MOLLY: Betrayal!

She pulls out the cork. She advances towards the dress.

MOLLY: One –

She pours a glug of the brown liquid onto the dress.

FREDDIE: No!

MOLLY: More –

MOLLY splashes another glug.

SEAN: (Irish accent): Molly, no no!

MOLLY: Betrayal!

She swirls the rest of the bottle over the dress.

FREDDIE and SEAN feverishly dab at the dress with handkerchieves. SERENA watches MOLLY. MOLLY picks up her phone, dials.

MOLLY: Sergey? Sergey Susemihl, is it yourself?

Molly McCloy.

Yes, Sergey, my brain is still finely honed, there. Listen I need to talk to you, Sergey, I want your help.

SERENA, SEAN, FREDDIE: No, Molly. Not Susemihl! No! Don't talk to Sergey Susemihl! Not that bastard. No, no, no!

Music.

Act 3 Scene 1

Following day, afternoon. The Cabinet Office. FREDDIE and SEAN (as ALBERT) are having tea. A lot of cake.

Music.

FREDDIE: The knickers have to be tiny, Albert. Scarcely there.

SEAN: *(as ALBERT)* After the former time –

FREDDIE: Look, I know, old man, Molly – well, you know, so highly strung and so forth, the Bastard's advice was very unclear.

SEAN: My art, my craft, even, monsieur, even my amour-propre, was, how you say, darted –

FREDDIE: Dented.

SEAN: Non, monsieur, my teeth, as you see, I eat this cake – my teeth are impeccable.

SEAN pulls both cheeks wide, dropping cake down his front.

FREDDIE: Dented, Albert. Biffed. Your pride, Albert, quite rightly –

SEAN: Destroyed. The filthy wine mademoiselle poured onto my exquisite silk –

FREDDIE: Look, absolutely devastating, a blow to us all, Albert, our little surprise for Molly blown off course by an Irish tornado –

SEAN: I think you say, we are all over sea –

FREDDIE: Well, that's it, the sea's the problem. Molly's very hot
               under the collar about checks in the Irish Sea.

SEAN: I do not recommend checks, monsieur. For
               mademoiselle's figure the line needs to flow down the,
               ah – qu'est-ce que le mot –

FREDDIE: No, old man, um – checks, you know – chappies in
               peaked caps with chits to tick off, – ah – VAT and all
               that, paperwork, wave you through, bon voyage and so
               on – look, Albert, I think the knickers will do the trick.

SEAN: Lingerie, with great sorrow, monsieur, we have to add
               on top the VAT. Even very small knick-knacks.

FREDDIE: For God's sake, Albert, whatever it takes. She's in a fury.
               I have to give her something.

SEAN: Petite lingerie française is not so much –

FREDDIE: The thought, old man, she'll know I'm thinking about
               her –

SEAN: She'll know what it is you are thinking.

FREDDIE: Exactly – contrition, make it up, stave off the rage.

SEAN: Maybe you are not thinking what she thinks you are
               thinking, monsieur.

FREDDIE cuts more cake.

FREDDIE: Women are not easy, Albert. Marvellous creatures in many ways, of course, but not easy.

SEAN: Mademoiselle is a little, shall we say, volatile.

FREDDIE: We shall say.

SEAN: She is above, and then she is below.

FREDDIE: That's it.

FREDDIE munches cake gloomily.

SEAN: She has flaming desires.

FREDDIE: Every now and then.

SEAN: She must eat one thing many times.

FREDDIE: You tailor chappies understand women. She won't stop eating Patum Peperium.

SEAN: *(shrugs Gallicly, quizzically)* Mais je comprends pas.

FREDDIE: Gentleman's Relish.

SEAN: Oh, mais oui, Woman is always be relished by un gentilhomme.

FREDDIE: Anchovy paste.

SEAN: Anchovy – mademoiselle has the passion for anchovy.

FREDDIE: By Jove, does she, can't stop. Like an animal.

SEAN: I offer you my salutations, monsieur.

FREDDIE: Well, Albert, merci, but –

SEAN: You have welded the sword of honour.

FREDDIE: No, wielded, you see –

SEAN: Mademoiselle est enceinte.

FREDDIE: Come again?

SEAN: The wedding dress – necessary, non?

FREDDIE: I don't know, Molly sometimes –

SEAN: How many months?

FREDDIE: Oh years, I'm sure.

SEAN: The maman of mademoiselle will insist you marry
             before the child sera arrivé.

FREDDIE: No child, Albert, what do you – ? No, Albert, no, I
             mean – ah, that's not –

Cake half-way to FREDDIE's lips.

FREDDIE: Oh Christ. Not again.

SEAN: Monsieur, I will prepare the samples. The atelier will
             be honoured to serve. The sherry is all over. Entente
             cordiale! The bells of mariage to ring. Ding, ding. Ding.
             Ding.

ALBERT goes.

FREDDIE: Yes, of course, ah – bottoms, up, old man.

The Bastard will kill me.

Act 3 Scene 2

Following day, lunchtime. The Cabinet Office. SERENA and MOLLY have just sat down. Sandwiches, a carafe of water and a thermos on the table.

MOLLY: Get rid of Smallwood.

SERENA: Sandwich, pet?

MOLLY: Take him out.

SERENA: He's a useful idiot. Try the salmon pâté.

MOLLY: We despised him at home, my mam said he was –

SERENA: Stupid and clingy?

MOLLY: Make him disappear. You can do it.

SERENA: Gentleman's Relish?

SERENA offers MOLLY a dish of crackers spread with Gentleman's Relish. MOLLY takes it eagerly.

MOLLY: 'Albert' drives me mad.

SERENA: Your idea, darling.

MOLLY: Just fire him. Let me report to you.

SERENA: You silly little goose, you know you can't do that. What we have is very strictly personal.

SERENA touches MOLLY's cheek. MOLLY pushes her hand away.

MOLLY: I'll get rid of him. Smallwood's a dead rat.

SERENA: Molly, dearest.

MOLLY: Don't touch me. I'm not for sale to you or anyone else!
                You people play games while my country lies bleeding,
                stabbed back and front, isn't it. Slashed by betrayal.

SERENA: Tiger.

MOLLY moves downstage, stands spotlit, facing audience.

MOLLY: Our women are hard, our men ground down, our
                families destroyed, our church derided, our great
                parades of loyalty to the Crown spat upon by people
                like you.

SERENA: Burn, my tiger.

MOLLY: Murderers run free in our country – filthy Catholic
                murderers attacked our house. The man who shot my
                Da sits fat in Stormont. I will fuck your Prime Minister
                until his head bursts and he understands once and for
                all that Ulster will not endure this betrayal of our nation.

MOLLY returns slowly to the table, spotlight fades.

SERENA: Come, sit next to me, this side.

MOLLY sits, complaisant, as if in a daze.

SERENA: Put your hands in your lap, my sweet. Close your eyes
                and open your mouth.

SERENA place a half-cracker spread with Gentleman's Relish on to MOLLY's tongue. MOLLY crunches it and licks her lips.

SERENA: I'll deal with Smallwood. Keep your eyes shut.

Another half-cracker.

SERENA: 'Albert' will upset the Prime Minister. I will get to hear
             of it.

Another half-cracker.

SERENA: Eyes shut.

Another half-cracker.

SERENA: 'Albert' will find his head on a guillotine block – just
             for you.

MOLLY bends forward for another mouthful. She licks her lips.

SERENA: The neck of your little rat will snap. Eyes tight shut.

SERENA watches MOLLY.

Music.

Act 3, Scene 3

Following night. Cabinet Office.

MOLLY:　　　　*(on her mobile, softly)* Sergey. Is it you, there?

[Molly. Are you safe?]

Of course I'm safe.

[Are we close?]

Getting closer.

[Do we need to get you out?]

Not yet. We need to deal with Riding Boots.

[Focus on Branscombe]

I am focussed on him. Listen, I want you to do something for me.

[Get rid of Branscombe?]

No, not Freddie, he's easy. This place is a pack of cards, you know it, don't you.

[The Bastard?]

Not the Bastard. He'll trip over himself there.

[He's powerful, no?]

Not worth your trouble.

[Anything for your mission is worth my trouble,
krasotka.]

Sergey, I appreciate that but listen to me, listen.

[We're very proud of you.]

Thank you. It's the black woman.

[I don't run her.]

You're not paying her? I thought she was one of yours.

[Not one of mine.]

She's in the way.

[She is not government.]

She's really creepy, she keeps – I can't make her do what
I need.

[She is protected by spies.]

Well get to her, she's running it here.

[Maybe you can seduce her.]

Sergey, I'm working my little tail off on Freddie, I can't –

[I don't know how.]

Whatever, I need you to remove her now.

[I said I don't have the means – how get rid of her?]

The usual. Polonium. Novichok. Only make it work.

[It needs many people.]

Well where are your people?

[We have not so many – finance cut-backs.]

Cut-backs? You mean I'm alone. On what you said you would pay?

[Do it for the mission. I can give you $5,000.]

I'm not doing it for that. Do you know what it's costing me? I get nothing from the DUP, nothing for being the Prime Minister's hot new flame and you're offering me – I need new outfits, I'm in the photos, I'm by his side, I'm carrying his child –

[Carrying? Inside you?]

Of course, inside me.

[Freddie knows?]

No, he doesn't know.

SERGEY: You betray my mission with him?

SERGEY's voice is suddenly on speakerphone. MOLLY is startled.

MOLLY: It's not about you, Sergey.

SERGEY: I need your brains, your courage.

MOLLY: I need you – to force the British to betray the Fenians again.

SERGEY: You tell me true?

MOLLY: Of course. Ulster must be necessary to the British.

Speakerphone off. MOLLY puzzled, then determined.

[You must do it now.]

We must be patient, isn't it. I need you to double my money.

[We have cut-back, Kiska.]

Double, you hear me there. Or I have the child and marry him.

Sergey?

[You would not do that to me]

I would. Double the money, get rid of this black policewoman and I'll make you feel you're king of the world.

Music.

Act 3 Scene 4

Following day, mid-morning coffee. Cabinet Office.

FREDDIE: I mean, ah, – I can't just, you know, fire the Head of MI5. They wouldn't let me.

MOLLY: You're Prime Minister, darling, we can do whatever we want, isn't it.

FREDDIE: I don't think she reports to me.

MOLLY: Everybody reports to you, Big Man. From the dirty little immigrants right up to me. Get rid of her.

FREDDIE: Someone said her boss is the Queen.

MOLLY: You talk to the Queen every week.

FREDDIE: Not about this.

MOLLY: About what, then?

FREDDIE: Ah, well, I can't tell you that, old girl –

MOLLY: What do you talk about? –

FREDDIE: Um – the weather, mainly – ah – what would happen if I fell under a bus, you know, strategic ifs and buts and all that sort of thing –

MOLLY: Ridinghard's bossy, she thinks she can tell you what to do.

FREDDIE: You've noticed –

MOLLY: Her Majesty, Ulster's Queen, takes you seriously, talks
             strategy with you and Dame Riding Boots thinks she
             can call the shots.

FREDDIE: She most certainly can't do that, by Jove –

MOLLY: So suggest to Her Majesty, when you have tea next
             week, that she sends Little Red Ridinghard back where
             she came from.

FREDDIE: The Bastard won't like it.

MOLLY: Fuck the Bastard.

FREDDIE: Says it's good optics.

MOLLY: What's that supposed to mean?

FREDDIE: No idea. Says it quite a lot and the Cabinet all nod at
             him. Look, forget about Serena, I've known her for
             ever, she's one of us really, doesn't look like it I know,
             but you know – look, have a chocolate biscuit.

MOLLY: She's not one of me. Her enforcers, and the enforcers
             before them, back into history, spied on us.

FREDDIE: No, Molly, she's a good egg, really, you know. Married a
             very close friend of an old Buller chum.

MOLLY: All the time, they double-cross us. Loyal unto death,
             we play straight, block the Fenians, defend the state
             and they shaft us, the snappers in the bushes, the
             under-cover double dealers –

FREDDIE: Molly, for heaven's sake – ah – you're upset by something. Look, Serena comes on a bit, I know, but she did well in the FO, good Iraq war, handling the Europeans and / all that –

MOLLY: She will not handle me! She creeps around me with her big hands and big tits, driving her wedge between us there.

FREDDIE: Darling Molly, you're imagining things, I understand, you know, how you feel. Look, Albert told me.

MOLLY: I want her out of here! Just do it.

FREDDIE: Albert told me, you know.

MOLLY: Albert can stitch up his mouth with his sewing machine.

FREDDIE: He said – ah –

MOLLY: He's one of hers, you know that, don't you –

FREDDIE: Look, he told me, as a tailor, you know, he understands women's bodies –

MOLLY: My body's my business.

FREDDIE: Well, I rather assumed, my little polecat, we were – ah, in a little, as it were, joint venture together in that department.

FREDDIE approaches MOLLY to embrace. She doesn't push him away.

MOLLY: That depends. Get rid of Bossyboots and we'll see.

FREDDIE: *(arms around her)* Albert pointed out, in his Gallic way, that you might have been a tiny bit, ah, you know, a touch careless –

MOLLY: And you weren't, is it? What do you think happens there, when you get over-excited, huff and puff and go plop inside me?

FREDDIE: Look, I know, birds and bees and so forth but it's your job –

MOLLY: My job? Is this an appraisal?

FREDDIE: Don't be silly, sweetheart – but, I can't have, you know, another one now –

MOLLY: It'll not be you that's doing the having there.

FREDDIE: The Bastard just won't wear it.

MOLLY: I told you fuck him, what's it to do with him?

FREDDIE: The optics, I expect, running the country and so on –

MOLLY: I want this child.

FREDDIE: Yes, darling, of course, but perhaps we could do it a bit later.

MOLLY: They don't wait – she's on her way.

FREDDIE: How do you know it's –

MOLLY: Of course it's a girl – and she'll fight for her country. You said we're forever, Freddie.

FREDDIE: We are, my dove, but we've not long been elected, and
             just at the minute, not for very long, I'm sort of, getting
             to grips with it, it seems – ah – rather a lot to do, you
             know –

MOLLY: I'll kill it then, shall I?

FREDDIE: God no, Molly, I don't mean –

MOLLY: Will we marry, just now?

FREDDIE: Yes, look, I've said many times –

MOLLY: Not to me.

FREDDIE: Yes, Molly, I must have done –

MOLLY: You've fucked me, but shall I kill it?

FREDDIE: Christ, you're going off the rails, stop talking about
             killing it.

MOLLY: You want our child.

FREDDIE: No. No, no, I mean yes, of course, we'll be a happy
             family and –

MOLLY: Renegotiate the Betrayal of Ulster.

FREDDIE: What?
             The Bastard doesn't care about Ulster.

MOLLY: I'll kill it then, is it?

FREDDIE: Enough of the killing! I went there, it's an awful place, people with thick hips and aggressive voices moaning on about their history, their loyalty, never vote the way you want, stick their noses into our trough year after year, it's an island, for God's sake, there's cold water all around it. They want to fight each other about the Pope then get on with it, I've got to – ah –, overturn the Civil Service, I think, then, you know, add on points for immigration – spend money like blazes – and then the Bastard wants me to –

MOLLY: I spoke to Sergey last night. He's asked me to marry him.

FREDDIE: You didn't say that, I mean, ah, you know, you didn't talk to Sergey.

MOLLY: We'll look after my daughter together.

FREDDIE: She's my child.

MOLLY: You've betrayed Ulster.

FREDDIE: Molly, darling, it's us, you know, just us, you and me and the dear little girl.

MOLLY: Sergey will look after us. He's strong. I call him my big Russian bear.

FREDDIE: But I'm your Freddie-teddy.

MOLLY: You spat upon my father's grave and just murdered your daughter.

FREDDIE: Nooo! You're upset, Molly, let's go and lie down.

MOLLY: Sergey is very upset.

Music.

Act 3, Scene 5

Following day, breakfast. Cabinet Office. SERENA is eating croissants and reading Horse and Hound. *SEAN is standing, nervously.*

SERENA: You're terminated tomorrow.

SEAN: *(wheedling)* N?

SERENA: One thing might save your job.

SEAN: I've tried to get Molly to give me her VAT receipts –

SERENA: Not / her VAT –

SEAN: As soon as I heard HMRC were coming in, I knew it.

SERENA: You've set this pregnancy rumour running.

SEAN: Sean Smallwood, I said to myself, Sean Smallwood, VAT will finish you. You know it, unless you keep on top of it, it rises up, a terrible tide of –

SERENA: Smallwood!

SEAN: Yes, N.

SERENA: Your wretched tailor has one last chance. 'Albert' must tell the Prime Minister he was mistaken – Molly is not bearing a child.

SEAN: Well, N, that's going to be very difficult, you see, my cousin, she's already bought the lovely material for the wedding dress, and –

SERENA: There will be no wedding.

SEAN: – and the lacework, her sister's old aunt across the
               border down there in Clones she still has the skills,

SERENA returns to Horse and Hound.

SEAN: – wonderful to behold, although her eyes are not so
               good, but it's not Catholic, you see, all started by the
               wife of a Church of Ireland pastor, way back, now –

SERENA: The Prime Minister is increasingly distracted by your
               nonsense.

SEAN: But you see, N, the very thing of it is I promised Molly's
               mam that I would look after her, the Free Presbyterians
               will damn her forever if the dear wee chit of a thing is
               born out of wedlock. Molly has to marry him.

SERENA: *(puts magazine down)* She is not pregnant.

SEAN: As her dressmaker, N, I can assure you –

SERENA: You are Smallwood, a low-grade civil servant. You are
               not a dressmaker!

SEAN: The Prime Minister doesn't know that. I, Albert
               Lefèvre, have his ear. Molly has his balls. He knows I
               know her body.

SERENA: Smallwood, know your place! Molly's body is above
               your pay-grade. And your pay is moments from
               ceasing altogether. I, N, order you 'Albert' to apologise
               to the Prime Minister and tell him you are wrong.
               Molly is not pregnant. Do you understand me?

SEAN: Yes, N.

SERENA: You tell me the Prime Minister trusts Albert Lefèvre.
             Convince me, or you're out.

SEAN: *(wheedling)* N –

SERENA: Get out!

SERENA turns back to Horse and Hound *and croissants. SEAN goes, tail between legs.*

Music.

Act 3 Scene 6

Same day, midnight. The flat above No. 11 Downing St. SERENA, in tuxedo, reading Vogue. *MOLLY comes in her dark red negligée.*

SERENA: Oh, my darling, you look fabulous.

MOLLY: I'm leaving tonight.

SERENA: Dressed like that? You'll be a sensation. I'll call the Daily Star.

MOLLY: Freddie's dithering.

SERENA: He does that.

MOLLY: He must marry me.

SERENA: Oh no he mustn't.

MOLLY: I'll have him completely.

SERENA: His wife doesn't think so.

MOLLY: My daughter and I –

SERENA: Your what?

MOLLY: My baby. My strong baby girl. She'll fight for Ulster.

SERENA: You're not pregnant. Smallwood's apologising to the PM.

MOLLY: I'm having this baby.

SERENA: It doesn't exist. It's a bloody nuisance. If this silly
            rumour gets out, the press will be all over it.

MOLLY: I am with child!

Long beat.

SERENA: You little bitch!

MOLLY: You dare call me –

SERENA: You've been completely unprofessional. Careless.

MOLLY: I've done my job.

SERENA: You are to distract and confuse him, not breed by him.

MOLLY: I've fucked his head off, so help me God, and I've not
            been properly paid.

SERENA: Getting pregnant by Freddie Branscombe – it's
            disgusting.

MOLLY: Smallwood gives me nothing, badgers me about VAT,
            you give me nothing, I've had no new outfits for three
            weeks, no decent shoes. I need maternity shapewear,
            softer lines –

SERENA: McCloy! You've gone way beyond your brief. Get rid of
            the foetus.

MOLLY, yelling, tears Vogue *from SERENA's hands, rolls it and beats
her head. SERENA backs away, MOLLY pursues her, comes close.
SERENA grabs her arms, pulls her towards her and kisses her firmly,
stopping MOLLY's noise.*

SERENA: Your body's mine. I don't want his rotten seed inside you. Flush it out! Clean him out of yourself! Come to me.

SERENA pulls MOLLY'S head down.

MOLLY: I hate you. Get your tits out of my face.

MOLLY forces SERENA's arms up.

MOLLY: God will punish you!

FREDDIE comes, in flannelette blue-striped pyjamas.

FREDDIE: Good lord!

MOLLY: *(struggling with SERENA)* Get her off me!

FREDDIE: I woke up, closed in for a cuddle, clasped / thin air –

MOLLY: *(beating her fists on SERENA's back)* Freddie!

SERENA: Prime Minister, rein in your filly.

FREDDIE: *(not knowing how to approach)* Look, ah – I say old thing –

MOLLY: Down, Ridinghard – onto your knees.

SERENA: Ow! McCloy / I warn you –

FREDDIE: Look, be careful –

MOLLY: Throw her out, Freddie.

FREDDIE: Well. I'm not so sure we've reached that point –

MOLLY: It's her or me, Freddie –

SERENA: McCloy, you report to me!

MOLLY suddenly lets SERENA go.

MOLLY: *(enraged, then distant)* I'm finished with you. Both of you. Ulster will fight on alone. My child will struggle under the rule of fickle ministers over the water, she will be loyal to Her Majesty the Queen and to the elders of her Free Presbyterian Church –

SERENA: *(standing)* She's going mad, Freddie. Take her to my office.

MOLLY: Sergey will take us in, orphans in the desert –

FREDDIE: OK darling, no need to talk of Sergey.

SERENA: Get her into my room, the leather sofa –

MOLLY: Don't touch us. We're going to Moscow –

FREDDIE: Come with me, dearest –

SERENA: Don't let her out of your sight. The Bastard will kill us if he hears her like this.

MOLLY: Sergey kissed me last night.

FREDDIE: What? Oh my God, no. Where?

MOLLY: On my lips.

FREDDIE: No, Molly.

MOLLY: He kissed me with his words. We talked long and long
            on the telephone there, as lovers do.

SERENA: Lovers! You betray me with that foxdung Susemihl?
            You'll regret that as long as you live.

MOLLY: He's my Russian bear. I love him.

SERENA: Tear out your tongue!

FREDDIE: Now, look – ah – hold your horses, Serena, Molly's –

SERENA: Get her out of my sight, thinks she can sell her body to
            the highest bidder. Well, she's oversold, she's horsemeat,
            her bones will boil down for glue!

FREDDIE: Look, we're going, I'm taking Molly back to bed – let's
            all calm down, a bit, look – ah, have a drink, Serena –

MOLLY: Ulster's revenge is hard and merciless –

FREDDIE: Yes dear, that's the way, come on, now, let's go and have
            a little cuddle, now –

MOLLY   Da! My Da! Give me strength –

FREDDIE goes, leading MOLLY away. SERENA clicks a remote.

Dialling tone.

SERENA: *(calling)* Sergey.

SERGEY appears on screen. He is wearing dark glasses and swimming trunks, lying on a lounger under a sun-ray lamp. He is speaking but silent.

SERENA: Sergey, you're on mute.

SERGEY searches around his screen.

SERENA: Unmute your mic.

            Oh, for heaven's sake.

            Bottom left.

SERGEY unmutes.

SERGEY: Yes, here is. Is that it, now? Serena, can you hear?

SERENA: Yes, Sergey, now I can hear.

SERGEY: Can you hear me, Serena?

Screen goes dark.

SERENA: I can hear you.

            Turn on the video.

            Jesus Christ.

SERGEY: I can see you, Serena. You are looking very nice.

SERENA: Turn on your fucking video!

            The little picture of a camera.

SERENA *(cont)*:   Next to the little picture of the microphone.

Give me strength.

SERGEY: Already you are very strong woman, Serena.

SERGEY suddenly appears on screen.

SERENA: You look grotesque. This is a business call.

SERGEY: The plane arrive at North Holt in two hours.

SERENA: Molly will be there.

SERGEY: What she will wear?

SERENA: Business dress. She is an employee of Her Majesty's government.

SERGEY: Her Majesty is lucky having beautiful staff.

SERENA: The Bastard wants Molly out of the way. She interferes with his optics.

SERGEY: Tell Bastard he make sure she is in car up to door of plane.

SERENA: It's the middle of the night.

The screen goes blank. SERENA picks up Vogue *once more.*

Music.

Act 3, Scene 7

A week later, breakfast time. Cabinet office. Breakfast uneaten. FREDDIE, unkempt, reading Daily Star.

SERENA comes, in severely smart business dress.

SERENA: The Cabinet is still waiting.

FREDDIE:

SERENA: Prime Minister, the Cabinet Secretary is irritated, there is urgent business.

FREDDIE:

SERENA: Freddie, pull yourself together!

FREDDIE: I couldn't stop her. It was as though she were fleeing some, you know, nightmare.

SERENA: You surprise me.

FREDDIE: Has she been in touch with you?

SERENA: She's your piece of fluff, not mine.

FREDDIE: A week. We've never been apart.

SERENA: A week in which government business is dangerously drifting and you haven't shaved.

FREDDIE: She's taken my child.

SERENA: There are others.

FREDDIE: Look, you know, the thing is, I – ah – I mean – I love
            her. Aphrodite came down, touched my lips –

SERENA: No hips. You need powerful hips for a good gallop.

FREDDIE: Molly means everything to me – look, she'll come back,
            won't she?

SERENA: Not unless you shower and shave. The loveable scruff
            look goes down well with the lower orders, but it's
            beyond tedious in government.

FREDDIE: I must have her.

SERENA: Cabinet is waiting.

FREDDIE: I want Molly. I want her body. I want my child.

SERENA: Get to work, the media are boiling up a –

Ringtone.

SERENA: Oh for heaven's sake.

*SERENA presses remote. TV screen appears. SERGEY and MOLLY,
seated under a sunshade, sunny seascape behind.*

SERENA: Sergey. You're an hour early. The Cabinet hasn't –

FREDDIE: Molly! Look – what, ah, I mean what, where are –

SERGEY: My friend! Freddie – long time, eh? Looking good.

MOLLY: It's terrible you look there now.

FREDDIE: Come back.

MOLLY: It's beautiful here.

SERGEY: Molly is wonderful woman. Is very clever and brave –
             you miss her trick –

FREDDIE: Sergey, old man, um – I mean, very good to see you
             and so forth –

SERGEY: You have no fear. I am father to the child.

FREDDIE: That child is 100% pure British Branscombe, I'm not
             having –

MOLLY: We're on honeymoon.

SERGEY leans in.

FREDDIE: Don't touch her, look, she's mine, take your hands off
             her –

FREDDIE lunges towards the screen.

SERENA: Stop it, Freddie. Molly Ivanovich Susemihl. She's
             moved on.

SERGEY: Here we have little time. Lunch soon. Serena – listen to
             my instructions. Tell Cabinet three things. One, build
             customs sheds along border between the Ulster and
             Irish – this my wedding present to my brilliant wife.
             Two, close port of Dover for long maintenance. You
             will see some Russian naval ship in English channel.

SERGEY *(cont)*:   Three, I want your Irish Littletree man to Foreign
              Minister.

SERENA: Smallwood? You're crazy, he's a worm. By the way he
              has to be in parliament.

SERGEY: Many MPs worms. Make him Lord Woodsomething.

SERENA: No, Sergey, not Smallwood.

SERGEY: Don't argue. Your husband's business in Russia may fail
              and your horses will starve. Sack Foreign Minister now
              – I don't know which he is.

FREDDIE: Listen, just back off here old man, I have a stonking
              majority and a world-beating mandate to lead this
              great –

              Molly is married to you?

SERGEY: Get old Conservative Friends of Russia gang together
              again – we had the great times, Freddie, didn't we. Put
              Whittingford in Cabinet again, Buckdale already there,
              good, Rifeking too old, Rosindere, you know – you get
              it going again, no?

FREDDIE: Molly! –

SERGEY: Listen my instructions, Freddie. Molly is here. Do as I
              say. Do as Serena say – she is powerful woman –

MOLLY: She's weird, Sergey, she –

SERGEY: Be quiet, Molly.

MOLLY: Be quiet, is it – don't –

SERGEY: We're speaking business – get ready for lunch.

MOLLY: Are you ready for me, Sergey? God is with us. He wants
            us to save my people. You and I will feed Ulster as I will
            nourish my beautiful daughter.

SERGEY: My Russian eagle wife – for you I do these things. For
            you Ulster will be rich, rest UK will be poor. Ireland
            will suffer, EU will break. People will kill each other
            again.

FREDDIE bangs on the screen.

FREDDIE: Send her back! Come to me! Look, OK, I'll get the old
            crowd together, we'll do business. But send her back!

SERGEY: Tell your Cabinet to do these things.

FREDDIE: It's very tricky – ah – difficult, the Bastard, you know,
            he's strong on ditching the Irish –

SERGEY: The Bastard is helping us here.

SERENA: You took him?

SERGEY: Poor guy mistake, stuck on same plane with my wife.
            Agreed to help development in Siberia   big roads,
            many stones.

SERENA: Long programme, Sergey?

SERGEY: Siberia very big.

FREDDIE: Bastard breaking rocks.

SERGEY: Very small.

SERENA looks at FREDDIE.

SERENA: Helpful.

FREDDIE: Helpful old girl, it's a bloody marvel.

MOLLY: Freddie, you're smiling.

FREDDIE: I am, my darling. So are you.

MOLLY: I've saved Ulster.

FREDDIE: They'll still complain. You look beautiful.

MOLLY: Sergey and I will bury the Nationalists for ever. We'll
             tear down the Catholic church.

FREDDIE: That's wonderful, my tigress. Come back to me.

SERGEY: Enough. Go shave. Order Cabinet to begin work.

FREDDIE: Look, I'll need, you know, a bit of time, festina lente
             and all that. I'm numero uno here, you know, but I'll do
             a deal with you, Sergey. Send me Molly. You keep the
             Bastard.

SERGEY: Forget Molly. Do what Serena tell you.

FREDDIE: Or what, you'll send in the Red Army?

SERGEY: I send you the Bastard.

Screen goes dark.

SERENA: He's serious, Freddie.

FREDDIE picks up a croissant, munches it thoughtfully.

FREDDIE: Molly's quite a handful, actually.

SERENA: Takes up a lot of our time.

FREDDIE: Couldn't get her off the Irish business. Never quite
             follow what she – I thought she was a Nationalist, you
             know, our nation, UK, Ulster and so on.

SERENA: No Freddie, Molly is what they call a Unionist.

FREDDIE: Yes, that's it, get together with the proper, you know,
             the Irish crowd in Dublin. We sorted all that out some
             time ago, I think, I believe I met him, unlikely name.
             Molly's very emotional about it.

Another mouthful of croissant.

FREDDIE   Not difficult to look at, though.

SERENA: So you say. I found her hard work.

FREDDIE: Old Sergey's a bit over the top.

SERENA: Sergey's not one of us, Freddie. The cousins are
             very stretched keeping tabs, much harder now. Our
             European friends are becoming circumspect. They
             didn't trust the Bastard.

FREDDIE chews.

FREDDIE: Weight off our mind?

SERENA: I can't let my horses starve.

FREDDIE: Good lord, no.

SERENA: He keeps Molly and the Bastard breaks rocks.

FREDDIE moves to the window, ruminates over Whitehall.

FREDDIE: I think it might be – ah – tempora mutantur, old girl.

Although Molly was – very – you know –

SERENA: Why don't you give Augusta a call.

FREDDIE: I say.

You know, I haven't seen her for –

SERENA: Very sound hips.

FREDDIE: No, you're right, she was rather good in the saddle. We had a marvellous trip once, riding across the Hungarian puszta.

SERENA: I know.

FREDDIE: I think her mother owned a place, fantastic country, lovely people. I wonder if she –

SERENA: More difficult now. The Hungarians are not as compliant as they were.

FREDDIE: I'm sure we know some good people.

SERENA: We do, but you put up a border. Like Miss No-hips.

FREDDIE: Molly's Sergey's problem. Back in the day, Augusta and I we just motored over there, wind in our hair, leapt on our horses and galloped off. Marvellous fun, we should get back to that.

Where's my phone –?

SERENA: Cabinet first.

FREDDIE: Yes, yes, of course, right, of course, I'll go and have a word –

SERENA: And you're going to say –

FREDDIE: Look, ah, I'll say that Molly –

SERENA: No need to mention Molly.

FREDDIE: No, ah – let me see – Russians a bit untrustworthy. Need to watch out, hold our horses on putting up borders, pleasures – and values, of course, values – of European civilization, common enemy, pull together on the beaches and so forth –

SERENA: Big majority –

FREDDIE: Yes, yes, that's it, massive majority, do what we like, good of the nation, back on track with old friends, just a tiff, getting rid of –

Maybe not see the Bastard for a while.

Sigh of relief all round.

SERENA: Chancellor Merkel?

FREDDIE: Ah. Yes. Diplomatic phone call. You know, clearing the air, Angela.

SERENA: The cousins would be very pleased.

FREDDIE: Little Foreign Office chappie can tell us his story again about the Chinese eating bats and pangolins.

             Look, brilliant idea about calling Augusta, I had my phone somewhere –

SERENA: Cabinet.

FREDDIE: Yes. Right. I'll tell them –

FREDDIE goes.

SERENA: Shave!

FREDDIE comes.

FREDDIE: What say?

SERENA: You're filthy. Wash. Shave. Buck up!

FREDDIE: Yes yes, instanter, wings of, of course, wings of.

FREDDIE goes. SERENA pours herself a very stiff brandy.

Music.

END